THE
100
GREATEST
CLIMBING AND
MOUNTAINEERING
BOOKS

Vertebrate Publishing, Sheffield
www.v-publishing.co.uk

THE 100 GREATEST CLIMBING AND MOUNTAINEERING BOOKS

Jon Barton

First published in 2020 by Vertebrate Publishing.

 Vertebrate Publishing
Omega Court, 352 Cemetery Road, Sheffield S11 8FT, United Kingdom.
www.v-publishing.co.uk

Front cover illustration by Andy Kirkpatrick from *Unknown Pleasures* (Vertebrate Publishing, 2018).

A CIP catalogue record for this book is available from the British Library.

ISBN **978-1-839810-28-2** (Paperback)
ISBN **978-1-839810-29-9** (Ebook)

10 9 8 7 6 5 4 3 2 1

Design and production by Jane Beagley.
www.v-publishing.co.uk

Vertebrate Publishing is committed to printing on paper from sustainable sources.

Printed and bound in Europe by Pulsio.

Introduction

Here is a list.

It contains 100 climbing and mountaineering books – something for you to idly think about while you're lashed to a belay stance. You might be thinking that it's a list of the greatest mountaineering books of all time ranked from 100 to one. It certainly isn't. Just as the pitch stretching ahead of you isn't the best climb in the world, or the hardest or the easiest. It's just a climb, and similarly here are some good books. You should read a few of them. Once you've reached the top of the climb, that is.

I would like to tell you that I've read them all. I haven't. I wish I could tell you I agree with the order. I don't. And I would like to tell you that my favourite five books of all time are on the list. Three of them aren't.

But it is a list, and as a genre of predominantly non-fiction, there are a few shockingly brilliant, possibly far-fetched books buried inside it.

The Methodology

The simple aim was to generate a list of the world's favourite mountaineering books. The basic rationale was this: if a book received a 'mention' then that equalled a 'vote'. No one mention was weighted above another – the book with the most votes got first, and so on. The following mention-gathering criteria was employed.

A competition win equalled one vote; shortlisting and special mentions also qualified for one vote. If a book was adapted into a movie – one vote. If a book received more than twenty 5-star reviews on *amazon.com*, one vote; and *amazon.co.uk*, also one vote. If a book made someone else's list, if it appeared on Goodreads, if it made the top fifty title searches on Google, and so on – all accounted for another vote.

Then, to start refining the list, I asked scores of climbers – as international as my address book would allow – to name their top five books. The only mentions not counted were where an author or publisher mentioned their own book; the only exception being me, as I had *The Endless Knot* in my top five which, technically speaking,

Left – Jack Roberts on the Ruth Glacier, 1978. © Simon McCartney.

is published by Vertebrate, but then it didn't get enough votes elsewhere so didn't make the cut anyway.

Where votes were tied, I went back to the internet to see what the book's footprint was in order to separate out one text from another.

Three points will be obvious to the statisticians out there. Firstly, the sampling is biased due to the influence of any regional algorithms at work in my web browsers, though I did use different browsers and search engines. Secondly, the results are predominantly in the English language (thanks Silvo Karo for your input) and ultimately my own bias was at play; books I know and recognise would jump out at me from obscure places and therefore get a few more votes. Thirdly, and sadly, the results favour older titles from a very early point – they just have more traction in the market. This means that books like Kelly Cordes's book *The Tower*, every bit as good as many in the top twenty, don't have the weight of time behind them. Similarly, *The White Spider*, which is at best an okay read, was everybody's favourite, despite few people really remembering why.

Basically, the list is just that: a list.

As Voytek Kurtyka pointedly told me:

'I can't switch my mind into musing about climbing books, especially as they didn't influence my brain so much. Certainly much less than the mainstream literature or the climbing itself or the music or just nature. By the way, do you know that it is a sin to put the arts on the ranking list?'

Female Writers and Protagonists

Amazon's top 100 mountaineering titles typically contains ninety-eight books by male writers. Of the two not written by men, one is Nan Shepherd's excellent *The Living Mountain*, while the other is a biography about a man written by Bernadette McDonald. Times they are a-changing, and with the publication of the anthology *Waymaking* – lots of votes but sadly ineligible – more female voices in the mountaineering genre are emerging. Give it five years and weigh the index based on modern publications and we will see a lot more female writers.

For the time being, enjoy the excellent works of McDonald, Mort, Shepherd, Moffat et al., because, after all – despite what Amazon says and against the tide of the sheer number of books published in the genre by men – a good few books by women made the cut, although sadly only one landed a spot in the top twenty-five.

Modern Classics

With publishing houses like Vertebrate Publishing, Mountaineers Books, Rocky Mountain Books, Les Éditions du Mont-Blanc, Guérin, Desnivel and Alpine Studio regularly publishing brilliant new mountain literature I would expect the top 100 to look very different if it had some sort of sales figures adjustment to analyse what people are buying and reading in the current market. Indeed, for any book published in the last ten years to make the top 100 is truly remarkable – and many others deserved to make the list. Talking to these publishers directly, some of their current top titles are:

- **Mountaineers Books** *Rising*, Sharon Woods; *My Old Man and the Mountain*, Leif Whittaker; *The Sharp End of Life*, Dierdre Wolownick.
- **Rocky Mountain Books** *Lord of the Abyss*, Paul Preuss; *Honouring High Places*, Junko Tabei and Helen Y. Rolfe; *Where the Clouds Can Go*, Conrad Kain.
- **Les Éditions du Mont-Blanc** *Muztagh Ata: le père des glaciers* (Muztagh Ata: the Father of Glaciers), Françoise Cadoux; *Nous étions immortels* (We Were Immortal), Maurizio Zanolla; *The 9th Grade*, David Chambre.
- **Guérin** *Je vous écris de là-haut* (I Write to You from Up There), Jean-Christophe Lafaille; *Double Espresso*, Cédric Sapin-Defour; *Raide Vivant* (Stiff Living), Paul Bonhomme.
- **Desnivel** *Bájame una estrella*, Miriam García Pascual; *Cita con la cumbre*, Juanjo San Sebastián; *Andando la vida*, Pati Blasco.
- **Alpine Studio** *Cento anni in vetta*, Daniele Redaelli; *Una vita tra le montagne*, Goretta Traverso; *La torre del vento*, Casimiro Ferrari.

The Greatest Writers

Authors with multiple entries include:

Peter Boardman
Walter Bonatti
Nick Bullock
Heinrich Harrer
Andy Kirkpatrick
Jon Krakauer
Bernadette McDonald
Reinhold Messner
Jim Perrin
Paul Pritchard
David Roberts
Eric Shipton
Joe Simpson
Joe Tasker
H.W. Tilman
Stephen Venables

Tourists

Halfway down the Ogre, while stormbound with broken ribs and pneumonia, Chris Bonington dryly said to what was left of Doug Scott, *'We're going to make a fortune out of this'*. Doug asked him how, and in a fit of coughing, Chris said, *'The Book! – The Book!'*

While it is typical for a mountaineer to have an adventure – possibly one where not everybody has the good fortune to return – and for the events to be scribbled down and sent to the publisher while fresh, it is also not unusual for great writers to pay our humble genre a visit and have a crack at a book. Macfarlane, Newby, Barker and Bowley; their books are all engaging, but they are not real climbers like you and me.

Authors without a full complement of toes almost got a sympathy vote.

The Collector's Choice

Collectors of mountaineering literature will buy any old yarn. They love one stormbound mountain epic as much as another, so they have an entirely different set of criteria by which they rank their 100 favourite books. I asked book collector Chris Harle what he looks for in a mountaineering book:

Scarcity: regardless of a book's age, scarcity drives the obsessive hunt for the 'holy grail' of mountain literature in second-hand bookshops, charity shops, book dealer websites and catalogues, auctions, eBay, and so on.

Condition is everything: you are always looking for a book that is in better condition than the one you already have.

Dust jackets: in some cases – particularly with books published before the Second World War – the dust jacket can account for fifty per cent of a book's value. This is due to the economic standards prevalent at the time when paper was generally of poor quality and dust jackets rarely survived undamaged.

First editions: as a general rule, first editions (first impression/printing) are more desirable.

Signatures: collectors tend to prefer author signatures written on the title page without any dedication or inscription to the book owner. Obviously, signatures of deceased authors on older books attract more value. It could be argued that certain modern books are scarcer unsigned!

Provenance: being able to trace the history of the book ownership adds interest – particularly if it belonged to a famous person or if they featured in the book.

'*And so from the hills we return refreshed in body, in mind and in spirit, to grapple anew with life's problems. For a while we have lived simply, wisely and happily; we have made good friends; we have adventured well.*' – **F.S. SMYTHE**, *The Mountain Top*

Noel Dwyer is another book collector. He had this to say:

> Mountaineering books are beautiful. They are about heroes. They describe the best of times and the very worst. They tell of the power of determination and of mountaineers who are never content. There is always a harder climb. These texts are valuable historical records of what it was like to be first to stand where no one has ever stood before. These books portray the beauty and the anger of nature. Turn the page and travel to the ends of the Earth. Read of times often nearly forgotten. Read of the glory and share the tears of loss.
>
> There will always be adventure for there will always be men and women for whom life is not life without challenges. Their stories will always be told and greatly appreciated and admired. Mountaineering books captivate and inspire. Read the word. Marvel at the photograph. Observe an added comment or a folded edge, a sign of a frustrating interruption. How amazing that these books, so small, can hold the world.

The Greatest Prize

The world's two most established prizes for the climbing and mountaineering genre are the Boardman Tasker Award for Mountaineering Literature and the Grand Prize at the Banff Mountain Book Festival. Winning both is tricky. Jerry Moffatt and Niall Grimes's *Revelations* and John Porter's *One Day as a Tiger* both won the Grand Prize at Banff, only to stumble against harsh judging in the Boardman Tasker Award. Whereas Simon McCartney's *The Bond* easily scooped the Boardman Tasker and won the Mountain Literature Award in Banff (a rare double), but not the Grand Prize. Only three authors and three books have done this double: Bernadette McDonald with *Freedom Climbers*, Paul Pritchard with *The Totem Pole* and Roger Hubank with *Hazard's Way*.

The Future of Mountaineering Writing

Everest books have always sold and always will. Even Vertebrate, which famously declared it wouldn't publish an Everest book, has somehow ended up with about a dozen of them – thankfully not all of them making the top 100. In the future, I think the good books will get better, and the bad books will get worse. It's no longer good enough to scribble down your epic, stick a cover photo on it, call it 'White Hell' and publish it. Today books need to compete with social media, with a thousand TV channels, YouTube and still their traditional enemy – the outdoors.

In recent years, the better publishing houses have been putting more and more thought into their mountain books; we've seen lovely designs, high production values, and interesting, new stories. Conversely, as a generation of baby-boomer mountaineers fade from view there has been a clamour to get it all down on paper and, encouraged by a rampant self-publishing industry, all sorts of tat has made it on to the pages of Amazon. Everybody has a book inside them, but in most cases that is exactly where it should stay.

What's In and What's Not

I've compiled a list of mountaineering narratives. Fundamentally each book is about climbing. What aren't included are anthologies, because I would insist on *The Games Climbers Play* winning.

Books primarily concerned with sitting on a coffee table haven't been included either – large format, heavily illustrated, indulgent books simply fill up the bookcase too quickly. Guidebooks – how-to and where-to – books are also excluded. Shit books didn't make the cut. Fiction was included, because after all who knows what's true and what isn't in some of our classic titles? It is enough effort working out who wrote some of them without questioning their truth. Ice as we know gets steeper over time, and handholds smaller.

Who Didn't Make the List?

Premier de cordée, Roger Frison-Roche's classic of French literature – better known in the English language as *First on the Rope* – is perhaps the greatest piece of climbing fiction ever written, and although now republished it had been long out of print during the list's research stage. Nick Williams' unsung gem *Jagged Red Line* got a handful of votes but not as many as it should, nor did Doug Scott's autobiography *Up and About*. Tony Howard's delightful account of his ascent of the Troll Wall and Trevor Braham's classic *When the Alps Cast Their Spell* also failed to make it. Reinhold Messner received a lot of votes for a lot of books, but his voting was spread widely so many of them didn't make the cut, and a few modern books very nearly made it, such as Alex Honnold's *Alone on the Wall*.

Have Your Say

Of course, you might not agree with some of the books in the list – I'd be very surprised if everyone did! So why not let me know what your top five mountaineering books are. Send me a message on Twitter (**@VertebratePub**) or email **info@v-publishing.co.uk** and let's keep the conversation going.

Right – *The Ogre*, Karakoram, Pakistan. © Ronnie Richards.

The Books

So, here they are. The 100 greatest climbing and mountaineering books. But remember: this is just a list.

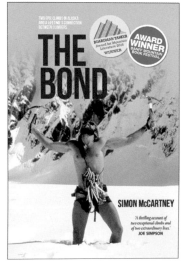

1   **The White Spider**
Heinrich Harrer

'Despite the grimness of much of what he is doing, Harrer communicates the irresistible joy of climbing as an antidote to the idea that climbers are masochistically trying to prove something to themselves.' – *THE SUNDAY TIMES*

2   **Touching the Void**
Joe Simpson

'Not only is it one of the most incredible survival stories of which I have heard, it is superbly and poignantly told and deserves to become a classic in this genre.' – CHRIS BONINGTON

3   **Conquistadors of the Useless**
Lionel Terray

'He is as much concerned with ecstasy and suffering as with technical achievement. He takes triumph and death in his stride, a dedicated professional writing with the gusto of an amateur.' – PADDY MONKHOUSE, *THE GUARDIAN*

4   **The Bond**
Simon McCartney

'A remarkable work of mountain writing that illuminates two legendary first ascents on Alaskan great walls: the North Face of Mt. Huntington and the Denali Diamond.' – RICK ACCOMAZZO, *ALPINIST*

5 **The Shining Mountain**
Peter Boardman

'It's a preposterous plan. Still, if you do get up it, it'll be the hardest thing that's been done in the Himalayas.'
– CHRIS BONINGTON

6 **Savage Arena**
Joe Tasker

'*Savage Arena* is a mad, exciting and dramatic tale of adventure, highly recommended for all mountain lovers.'
– MARK HORRELL, *FOOTSTEPS ON THE MOUNTAIN*

7 **Annapurna**
Maurice Herzog

'Those who have never seen the Himalayas ... will know that they have been a companion of greatness.'
– *THE NEW YORK TIMES*

8 **Into Thin Air**
Jon Krakauer

'*Into Thin Air* ranks among the great adventure books of all time.' – *WALL STREET JOURNAL*

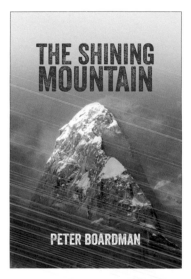

THE SHINING MOUNTAIN

PETER BOARDMAN

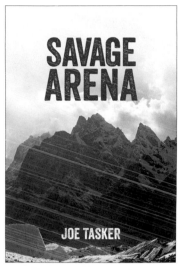

SAVAGE ARENA

JOE TASKER

VINTAGE **HERZOG**

ANNAPURNA

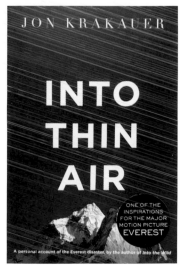

JON KRAKAUER

INTO THIN AIR

ONE OF THE INSPIRATIONS FOR THE MAJOR MOTION PICTURE EVEREST

A personal account of the Everest disaster, by the author of *Into the Wild*

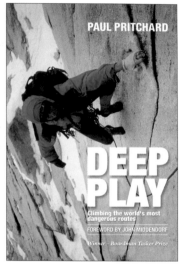

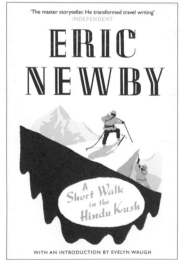

9   **The Ascent of Rum Doodle**
    W.E. Bowman

    A 'gem of social parody, suppressed masculinity and
    sustained comedy.' – KIM BUNCE, *THE GUARDIAN*

10 **Deep Play**
    Paul Pritchard

    'It is a remarkable book. It is a love letter to the mountain,
    an obituary for lost friends, a Joycean study of a
    community. Most of all, in its roughshod description
    of thrills and achievement, adventure and comradeship
    ... it's an explanation of a way of life.' – SABINE DURRANT,
    THE GUARDIAN

11 **No Picnic on Mount Kenya**
    Felice Benuzzi

    'Benuzzi's sketches and his glorious writing and humour
    make this an incomparable tribute to camaraderie and
    daring.' – JANE MANASTER, *SAN FRANCISCO BOOK REVIEW*

12 **A Short Walk in the Hindu Kush**
    Eric Newby

    'The most successful travel writer of his generation.
    It's impossible to read this book without laughing aloud.'
    – *THE OBSERVER*

13   **Beyond the Mountain**
      Steve House

      'A gripping tale in the great alpine tradition.'
      – YVON CHOUINARD

14   **One Man's Mountains**
      Tom Patey

      'Patey offers vigorous description, of men … as much as
      of mountains, informed by a lively awareness of one thing.
      Climbing up icefields and rocks is a completely ridiculous
      thing to do.' – RONALD TURNBULL, *UKCLIMBING.COM*

15   **The Mountains of My Life**
      Walter Bonatti

      'At the end of the climbing chapters one is left with an
      image of Bonatti as perhaps the last knight from the
      Golden Age of Alpine Mountaineering.' – PAUL DONNELLY,
      IRISH MOUNTAINEERING CLUB

16   **Fiva**
      Gordon Stainforth

      'A wonderful, nostalgic, gripping, classic yarn with great
      humour.' – JOE SIMPSON

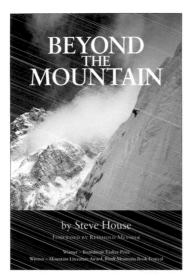

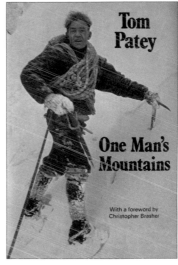

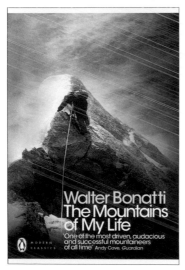

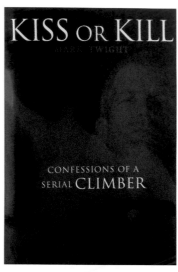

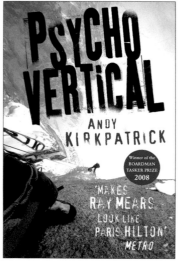

17 **Starlight and Storm**
Gaston Rébuffat

'One of the great climbers of all time ... who has
discovered through the medium of mountains the
true perspective of living.' – SIR JOHN HUNT

18 **Kiss or Kill!**
Mark Twight

'This is literature about the soul of alpinism, not a blow-
by-blow account of climbing drudgery from some tourist
peak bagger.' – *ROCK & ICE*

19 **Psychovertical**
Andy Kirkpatrick

'Makes Ray Mears look like Paris Hilton.' – *METRO*

20 **The Last Blue Mountain**
Ralph Barker

'The last part of the book is merciless to the feelings
of the reader.' – *THE DAILY TELEGRAPH*

21 **Learning to Breathe**
Andy Cave

'Doubtless, it will be regarded as the Billy Elliot book of mountaineering, but [Andy's] life and achievements are so much greater than that.' – **JOE SIMPSON**

22 **This Game of Ghosts**
Joe Simpson

'This book is not so much about why we climb – Simpson can't answer that for himself, much less the rest of us – but why we take such risks for such fleeting rewards. Overall this is a great book – perhaps the most honest bit of climbing writing I have read.' – **JOHN SHERMAN**, *CLIMBING*

23 **Freedom Climbers**
Bernadette McDonald

'As most high-altitude climbing becomes routinely commercial, the story Bernadette McDonald tells couldn't come at a better moment.' – **ED DOUGLAS**, *UKCLIMBING.COM*

24 **One Day as a Tiger**
John Porter

'A book on climbing both humorous and perceptive, as close to the essence of our life as you can get.'
– **DOUG SCOTT**

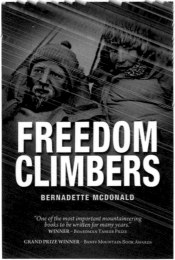

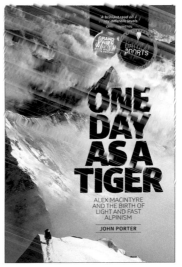

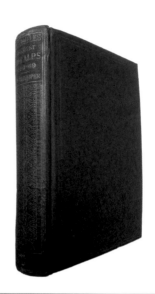

25 **Everest, The West Ridge**
Tom Hornbein

'Not only did Hornbein play a crucial role in one of the most extraordinary accomplishments in the history of mountaineering, his account of the feat is one of the finest things ever written about this peculiar, hazardous, and uncommonly engaging pursuit.' – JON KRAKAUER

26 **Scrambles Amongst the Alps in the Years 1860–69**
Edward Whymper

I was urged to Mont Pelvoux by those mysterious impulses which cause men to peer into the unknown.

27 **Feeding the Rat**
Al Alvarez

'That mountain of details about climbing a mountain – details that would ground you in anyone else's hands – takes you climbing.' – JANE KRAMER

28 **Nanga Parbat Pilgrimage**
Hermann Buhl

'About the life of whom I consider my "mountain father".'
– KURT DIEMBERGER

29 **The Villain**
Jim Perrin

'These stories are described with the drollness, skill and
attention to detail we expect from Perrin, who shines
through his own text – acute, sly, human and affable
– as concerned as ever that we view climbing as
the morally complex metonym of our humanity.'
– M. JOHN HARRISON, *THE GUARDIAN*

30 **The Climb**
Anatoli Boukreev

'This powerful tale will make climbers who are interested
in scaling Everest think twice about donning their boots.'
– *PUBLISHERS WEEKLY*

31 **A Slender Thread**
Stephen Venables

'Venables is one of the best climbers in the world, and
one of the best writers about climbing … Read it, but
be careful. You may never be content just to climb the
stairs again.' – JULIAN CHAMPKIN, *MAIL ON SUNDAY*

32 **Into the Silence**
Wade Davis

'Assiduously researched, this defining, and exhaustive,
book is not for the faint of interest. Set aside a season
for this extraordinary expedition.' – HOLLY MORRIS,
THE NEW YORK TIMES

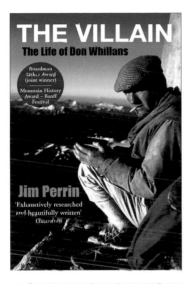

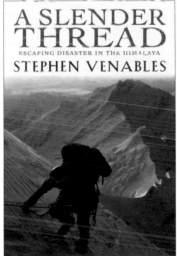

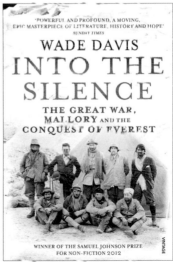

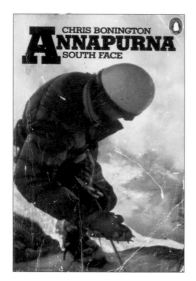

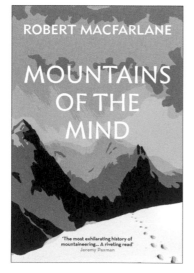

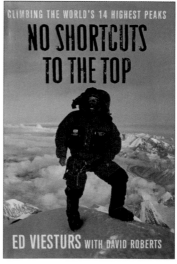

33 **Annapurna South Face**
Chris Bonington

'In addition to giving credit where credit is due, Bonington
provides an unmistakable sense of the difficulty and
complexity of a major mountaineering expedition.'
– *THE MOUNTAINEERING REVIEW*

34 **Blank on the Map**
Eric Shipton

'*Blank on the Map* is perhaps the book of his which best
encapsulates the spirit of exploration, and describes
an expedition to the Shaksgam area of the Karakoram
mountains just north of K2 in 1937.' – **MARK HORRELL**,
FOOTSTEPS ON THE MOUNTAIN

35 **Mountains of the Mind**
Robert Macfarlane

'The transformation of mountain landscapes in the
European imagination was an astonishing reversal and
that process has rarely been explored so effectively
as Robert Macfarlane does in *Mountains of the Mind*.'
– **ED DOUGLAS**, *THE GUARDIAN*

36 **No Shortcuts to the Top**
Ed Viesturs with David Roberts

'Viesturs has retrieved his share of bodies, and grieved
at the losses, but if he feels any guilt about surviving,
he doesn't say so.' – **JOHN ROTHCHILD**, *THE NEW YORK TIMES*

37 **Everest the Cruel Way**
Joe Tasker

'A grim story of eight comrades, with slender resources
— crack mountaineers all — undertaking a cruel
task with high resolve, but who are worn down by
the unremitting, bitter cold, by their decision not to
use oxygen equipment and, finally, by their formless
organization which the group labels "democracy."'
— TOM HOLZEL, *AMERICAN ALPINE CLUB JOURNAL*

38 **Sacred Summits**
Peter Boardman

'Pete Boardman is a very engaging writer with a great
deal of humility [...] His books are as much about the
people as the mountains, and he has a rare skill of
beig able to bring characters to life.' – MARK HORRELL,
FOOTSTEPS ON THE MOUNTAIN

39 **The Hard Years**
Joe Brown

'The climber of genius, who led the way to new
concepts of what might be possible on rock.'
— *TIMES LITERARY SUPPLEMENT*

40 **Space Below My Feet**
Gwen Moffat

'From the first page to the last I was enchanted by the
book, my own wanderlust being excited by her words of
freedom and emancipation.' – EMILY PITTS, *WOMEN CLIMB*

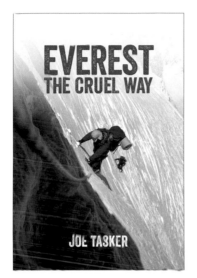

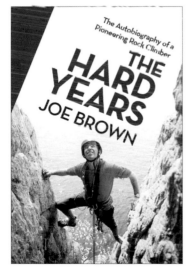

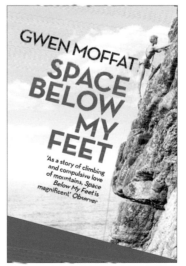

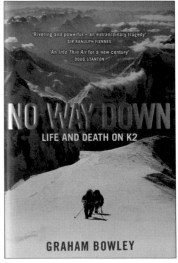

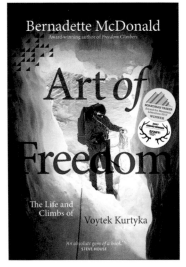

41 **Climbing Days**
Dorothy Pilley

'Climbing Days ... is an acknowledged classic of the mountaineering canon. Gracefully written, by turns sensitive and entertaining, it brilliantly evokes the subtle beauty of the sport and the intense power it can exercise over its practitioners.' – **DAVID MAZEL**, *MOUNTAINEERING WOMEN: STORIES BY EARLY CLIMBERS*

42 **Minus 148°**
Art Davidson

'*Minus 148°* is a riveting adventure story, one that thanks to the shared journals delivers deeper insights into what tensions and self-analysis develop as one struggles through incredible cold to reach the roof of the continent.' – **KURT REPANSHEK**, *NATIONAL PARKS TRAVELER*

43 **No Way Down**
Graham Bowley

'In *No Way Down: Life and Death on K2*, the *New York Times* reporter Graham Bowley relies on a copious study of the events and interviews with survivors and families to artfully and assiduously piece together an account of a fractious day in brutal real time.' – **HOLLY MORRIS**, *THE NEW YORK TIMES*

44 **Art of Freedom**
Bernadette McDonald

'[McDonald] carefully opens him up to make observations that are some of the most relevant ever written about the nature of climbing.' – **JOHN PORTER**, *UKCLIMBING.COM*

45 **The Mountain of My Fear**
David Roberts

'Roberts' trademark was – and is – unflinching honesty.
He tells it like it is. He also tells it beautifully, in a distinctive,
flawless voice that leaves the rest of us who write about
the sport feeling an uncomfortable mix of admiration
and bald envy.' – JON KRAKAUER

46 **The Crystal Horizon**
Reinhold Messner

*The notion of climbing the mountain again, and this
time alone, was for a long time mere fantasy. Only
when the day-dreams … outgrew fancy, did there
begin an exciting year in my life.*

47 **Eiger Dreams**
Jon Krakauer

'The author of *Into Thin Air* has taken the literature of
mountains onto a higher ledge.' – *THE NEW YORK TIMES*

48 **Revelations**
Jerry Moffatt and Niall Grimes

'Moffatt and Grimes have done climbing history a service
in setting down the story of UK climbing in the "dole
era" of the 1980s – a story that was quickly becoming
forgotten.' – *BANFF MOUNTAIN BOOK FESTIVAL*

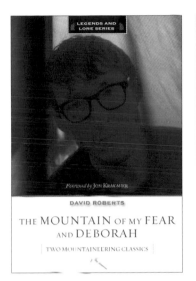

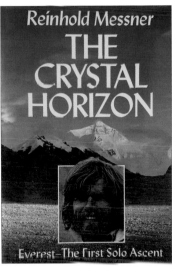

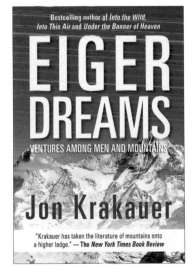

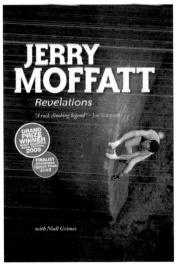

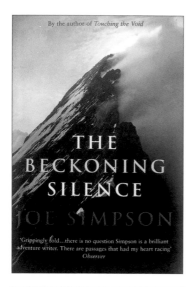

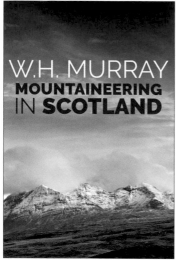

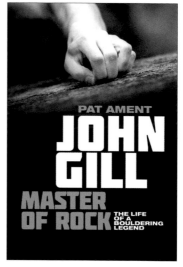

49   **The Beckoning Silence**
Joe Simpson

'There are passages that had my heart racing and his descriptions of the inner uncertainties that dog the climber – and climbing partnerships – are among the most convincing I have ever read.' – PETER BEAUMONT, *THE GUARDIAN*

50   **In Monte Viso's Horizon**
Will McLewin

'In a beautifully produced volume, he intersperses personal accounts of the ascents with reflections on diverse issues such as diminishing wilderness, food and equipment, and soloing.' – STEPHEN GOODWIN, *THE INDEPENDENT*

51   **Mountaineering in Scotland**
W.H. Murray

'If you could distil inspiration for exploring the Scottish mountains into a single volume – seasoned with a hefty pinch of romanticism and even mysticism – *Mountaineering in Scotland* is probably what you'd end up with.' – ALEX RODDIE, *UKHILLWALKING.COM*

52   **John Gill: Master of Rock**
Pat Ament

'A solid read from the father of bouldering. It shows just how he influenced many of the greats.' – MANSEL KERSEY, *AMAZON.CO.UK*

53 **Let's Go Climbing!**
Colin Kirkus

'Would make the parents of any middle-class 1940s schoolchild happy to send their adorable little bunny off to tackle the Eigerwand.' – COLIN WELLS

54 **K2, Triumph and Tragedy**
Jim Curran

'A gripping story that belongs with the classics of mountaineering.' – *PUBLISHERS WEEKLY*

55 **My Climbs in the Alps and Caucasus**
A.F. Mummery

'Mummery's book – plus Mary's contribution – is the defining account of what's called the Silver Age of Alpine Mountaineering.' – RONALD TURNBULL, *UKCLIMBING.COM*

56 **Nanda Devi**
Eric Shipton

When a man is conscious of the urge to explore, not all the arduous journeyings, the troubles that will beset him and the lack of material gains from his investigations will stop him.

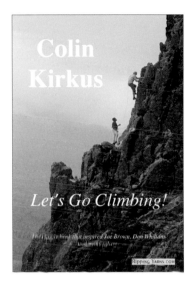

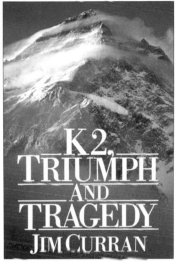

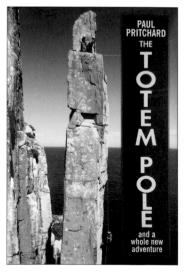

57 **The Push**
Tommy Caldwell

'*The Push* stands out as a genuine achievement in its own right – and is about much more than just climbing.'
– **PAUL SAGAR**, *THE GUARDIAN*

58 **Summits & Secrets**
Kurt Diemberger

'In a climbing life of many highs, his humanity and wonder at the natural world shines through – it's a life-affirming read.' – *AMAZON.CO.UK REVIEW*

59 **On the Heights**
Walter Bonatti

The mountains have rules. They are harsh rules, but they are there, and if you keep to them you are safe. A mountain is not like men. A mountain is sincere. The weapons to conquer it exist inside you, inside your soul.

60 **The Totem Pole**
Paul Pritchard

'Pritchard's story is a cautionary one. We should be careful when we tread upon high places. We are not gods, and we tempt their patience.' – **DAVID HALE**, *AMERICAN ALPINE JOURNAL*

61 **The Playground of Europe**
Leslie Stephen

'A fascinating description of British first ascents
in the Alps.' – *AMAZON.CO.UK REVIEW*

62 **Total Alpinism**
René Desmaison

'It is like sitting down with one's best pal and
listening to him tell about his latest wild climb.'
– *AMERICAN ALPINE JOURNAL*

63 **Seven Years in Tibet**
Heinrich Harrer

'Some books, like some mountains, are lonely and
unrivalled peaks. This is one of them.' – *THE ECONOMIST*

64 **Annapurna, A Woman's Place**
Arlene Blum

'Annapurna: A Woman's Place is both a devastating
and triumphant account of the '78 expedition. ...
The writing is superb, fast-paced, and reflective.
Even if the reader has zero experience with high
altitude climbing (or any climbing), this book is
a beautiful and harrowing adventure story sure
to impress.' – **SARAH SENTZ**, *MISADVENTURES*

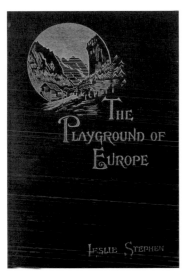

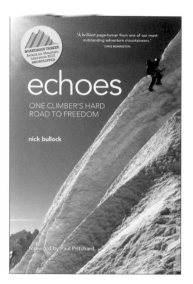

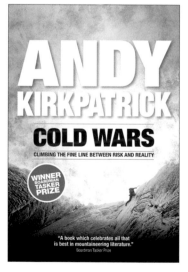

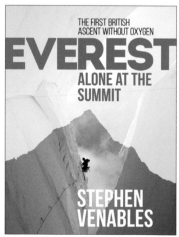

65   **Echoes**
Nick Bullock

'Bullock writes with a rare candour not just about his
climbs but also about his political education in a violent
world.' – **PETER BEAUMONT**, *THE OBSERVER*

66   **The Black Cliff**
Peter Crew, Jack Soper and Ken Wilson

'This is a rich collation of diverse stories, images and
history, that together synthesises the many people and
experiences coagulating into several decades of mad
adventures.' – *AMAZON.CO.UK REVIEW*

67   **Cold Wars**
Andy Kirkpatrick

'Andy is one of the funniest of Britain's top climbers and
represents what is the best in modern British climbing:
boldness, innovation, sense of humour, irreverence,
commitment and an appetite for risk.' – **CHRIS BONINGTON**

68   **Everest, Alone at the Summit**
Stephen Venables

'Venables – bespectacled, learned, self-effacing,
madly daring – is the poster boy of all who believe
climbing is more than just brute force and pitons.'
– **ROBERT TWIGGER**, *THE GUARDIAN*

69 **Deborah**
David Roberts

'As Dave gratefully acknowledges, there were many
good moments of warmth, joy and brotherhood.
The difficulty for a writer about such moments is
that it seems to be a law of language that happiness,
like goodness, is almost impossible to describe,
while conflict, like evil, is all too easy to depict.
A most fascinating book.' – *THE NEW YORK TIMES*

70 **Eiger Direct**
Peter Gillman and Dougal Haston

'If you are a long-time armchair fan of mountaineering
literature, this is an essential volume.' – *AMAZON.COM
REVIEW*

71 **Fallen Giants**
Maurice Isserman and Stewart Weaver

'*Fallen Giants* is the book of a lifetime for its authors,
an awe-inspiring work of history and storytelling ...
Keep it on a low shelf, where boys and girls can
discover it and start dreaming of their own expeditions.'
– **BRUCE BARCOTT**, *THE NEW YORK TIMES*

72 **The Living Mountain**
Nan Shepherd

'This is sublime, in the 18th-century sense,
when landscapes like these were terrifying.'
– **NICHOLAS LEZARD**, *THE GUARDIAN*

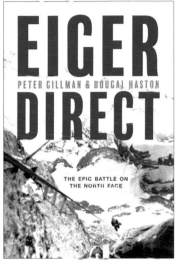

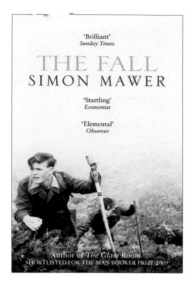

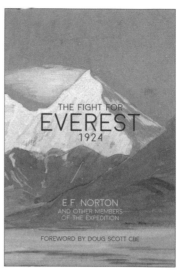

73 **The Fall**
Simon Mawer

'Simon Mawer is as fearless as his climbers and has
boldly produced a novel that is at once a gripping
yarn and something more meditative.' – **PATRICK GALE**,
THE INDEPENDENT

74 **The Fight for Everest 1924**
E.F. Norton

'If Everest's reputation has become tarnished and
diminished to one of high-altitude tourism then read
this book and recapture the unadulterated essence of
the challenge.' – **MIKE JACOB**, *SCOTTISH MOUNTAINEERING
CLUB JOURNAL*

75 **The Ascent of Nanda Devi**
H.W. Tilman

'And he was also a wonderful writer   one of those
whose style is highly distinctive and amazingly
effortless.' – **GAVIN ATKIN**, *IN THE BOATSHED*

76 **Gervasutti's Climbs**
Giusto Gervasutti

'Through the stimulating, sometimes nerve-wracking
descriptions of his Laocoon-like struggles with the
mountains and through the reflective pauses in
the narrative, Gervasutti develops an aesthetics of
mountaineering which is not unlike some eighteenth
and nineteenth century aesthetics of fine arts.'
– **GARY HARRISON**, *CLIMBING*

77 **The Tower**
Kelly Cordes

'A mix of investigative journalism with history and
great story telling, Kelly Cordes brings you to the
drama and makes you think about one of the most
beautiful mountains on Earth trashed by egos.'
— *THE CAMPSITE BLOG*

78 **K2, The Savage Mountain**
Charles S. Houston and Robert H. Bates

'Here is a great story, simply and grippingly told, which
the glory of Everest should not be allowed to obscure.'
— *THE NEW YORK TIMES*

79 **Where the Mountain Casts its Shadow**
Maria Coffey

'Coffey begins where Jon Krakauer left off. His
characters strive, suffer and vanish "into thin air".
This compelling book offers voices from the other
side of the mountaineering story – those left behind.'
— **KENNETH R. WEISS**, *LOS ANGELES TIMES*

80 **The Ordinary Route**
Harold Drasdo

'Drasdo calls himself an alternative historian, a village
philosopher; both epithets are modest. For me he is the
most enjoyable writer on climbing today.' – **ANDY POPP**,
HIGH

THE TOWER

A CHRONICLE OF CLIMBING AND CONTROVERSY ON CERRO TORRE

KELLY CORDES

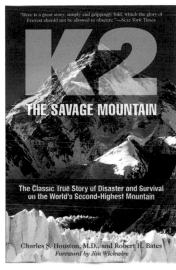

"Here is a great story, simply and grippingly told, which the glory of Everest should not be allowed to obscure."—*New York Times*

K2

THE SAVAGE MOUNTAIN

The Classic True Story of Disaster and Survival on the World's Second-Highest Mountain

Charles S. Houston, M.D., and Robert H. Bates
Foreword by Jim Wickwire

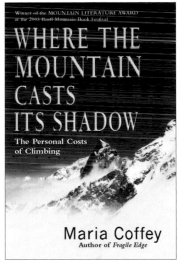

Winner of the MOUNTAIN LITERATURE AWARD at the 2003 Banff Mountain Book Festival

WHERE THE MOUNTAIN CASTS ITS SHADOW

The Personal Costs of Climbing

Maria Coffey
Author of *Fragile Edge*

THE ORDINARY ROUTE

Harold Drasdo

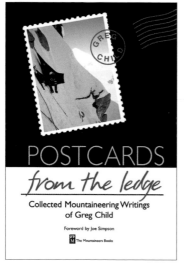

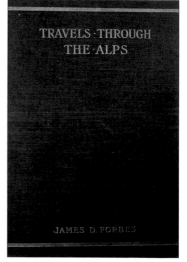

81 **The Climb up to Hell**
Jack Olsen

'One of the best accounts of true high mountain
adventure ever written.' – *TREVANIAN*

82 **The Seventh Grade**
Reinhold Messner

'It's an impressionistic piece, a haughty sandwich
of interior monolog with old-fashioned climbing
narrative' – **GEORGE LOWE AND MARSHALL RALPH**,
AMERICAN ALPINE JOURNAL

83 **Postcards from the Ledge**
Greg Child

'*Postcards from the Ledge* finds Child at the height of his
powers. Rare is the case of a climber still in the vanguard
of ascent who achieves a balanced perspective on the
glorious folly of mountaineering, and for good reason.'
   DAVID ROBERTS, *AMERICAN ALPINE JOURNAL*

84 **Travels Through the Alps of Savoy and
Other Parts of the Pennine Chain**
James D. Forbes

*Men travel from a great variety of motives, and they publish
their travels perhaps from a still greater. The manner
of travelling, and the forms of publication are equally
diverse, and mark strongly the features of the age.*

85 **Native Stones**
David Craig

'A meditation on and celebration of the sport written by a poet who is an accomplished amateur climber ... *Native Stones* is exceptional.' – CHAUNCEY LOOMIS, *LONDON REVIEW OF BOOKS*

86 **South Col**
Wilfrid Noyce

'Read Hunt to learn how to be the first to achieve the summit of Mt. Everest. Read Noyce to experience that climb.' – *GOODREADS REVIEW*

87 **Tides**
Nick Bullock

'Young want-to-be-sponsored climbing bums beware, all is not glory on this path, for as well as the slippery sea-cliff holds, long runouts and Himalayan storms lie other perils: self-questioning, angst at ageing, failed relationships, and a search for meaning.' – IAN WELSTED, *BANFF MOUNTAIN BOOK COMPETITION*

88 **Clouds from Both Sides**
Julie Tullis

'The life of Julie Tullis was very much the stuff of a BBC haut-montain opera. [She] attained extraordinary heights in the four years of her "second life", before succumbing to altitude and exposure on K2.' – **PATTI HAGAN**, *THE NEW YORK TIMES*

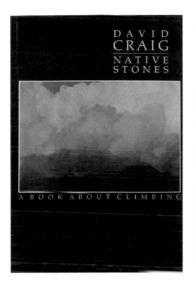

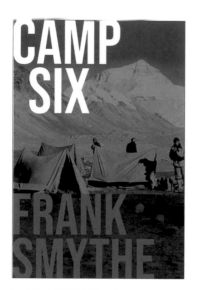

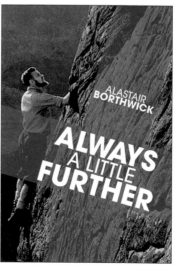

89 **Camp Six**
Frank S. Smythe

'You can't help but be amazed at what they did under
the most challenging conditions imaginable ... It really
puts today's Everest books in the proper perspective.'
– *AMAZON.COM REVIEW*

90 **Menlove**
Jim Perrin

'Perrin has, in spite of himself, allowed the reader
to draw an alternative picture of Menlove's tragedy,
with its origins in character rather than situation.
Highly recommended, especially to Perrinophobes.'
– **A.V. SAUNDERS**, *ALPINE JOURNAL*

91 **No Map Could Show Them**
Helen Mort

'Mort's *No Map Could Show Them* is an important
book in the way it embraces a range of female
narratives. Mort looks at fearlessness and fear, strength
and weakness, not settling for a simpler story, but
engaging with a variety of perspectives over time.'
– **ISABEL GALLEYMORE**, *THE LONDON MAGAZINE*

92 **Always a Little Further**
Alastair Borthwick

'A vivid memoir of a decade's carefree and impetuous
stravaiging through the Scottish Highlands.' – **JIM PERRIN**,
THE GUARDIAN

93 **Life and Limb**
Jamie Andrew

'The gripping story of his accident and recovery
develops into a more complex account of the family
and relationship loyalties which climbers routinely
betray in search of the ultimate high.'
– JONATHAN HEAWOOD, *THE OBSERVER*

94 **The Ogre**
Doug Scott

'It is one of the greatest mountaineering survival tales
never told.' – NICHOLAS HELLEN, *THE SUNDAY TIMES*

95 **The Alps from End to End**
William Martin Conway

'There was room for a book which should tell intending
travellers with only a limited holiday how to traverse the
"Alps from End to End".' – *THE DAILY NEWS*

96 **The Calling**
Barry Blanchard

'In the climbing world, reputation is everything. And
in that world, Canadian hardman Barry Blanchard
might possess the very best.' – GREGORY COUCH,
THE WALL STREET JOURNAL

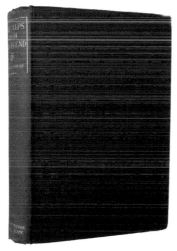

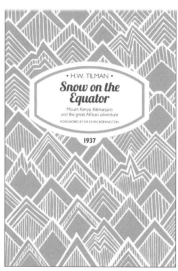

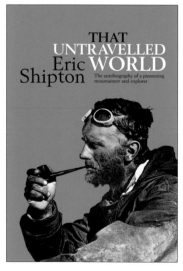

97   One Green Bottle
Elizabeth Coxhead

'Possibly one of the most iconic novels about rock-climbing ever written.' – **KATY STOCKS**, *WOMEN CLIMB*

98   Snow on the Equator
H.W. Tilman

'Snow on the Equator, which is more of a travel than a mountaineering book, has a neat style and often delightful humour.' – *AMERICAN ALPINE JOURNAL*

99   That Untravelled World
Eric Shipton

'This is the sort of life some of us dream about, but very few are lucky enough to have.' – *AMAZON.CO.UK REVIEW*

100   Call-out
Hamish MacInnes

'This book takes you into the heart of rescues: the tragedy, the triumph of recovering a badly injured walker or climber.'   **DAVID WHALLEY**

Climb when ready!